Natural Disasters

A CHAPTER BOOK

BY MADELINE BOSKEY

SCHOLASTIC INC.

New York Toronto London Auckland Sydney
Mexico City New Delhi Hong Kong Buenos Aires

For Cole

ACKNOWLEDGMENTS

The author would like to thank all those who gave their time and knowledge to help with this book. In particular, special thanks go to Dr. Jeffrey Masters, Chief Meteorologist, the Weather Underground, Inc.; Herb Stein, Severe Weather Scientist, University of Oklahoma; Michael J. McPhaden, Senior Research Scientist, Pacific Marine Environmental Laboratory, Seattle, Washington.

ISBN 0-516-24467-1

12 11 10 9 8 7 6 5 4   4 5 6 7 8/0

Printed in the U.S.A.   61

First Scholastic Book Club printing, September 2003

CONTENTS

INTRODUCTION

In this book, you will read about **disasters** that take place in nature. There are storms that can knock down trees. Some storms are so strong they can lift a train off the tracks. There are mountains that explode in fire.

Disasters put people and their belongings in danger. That's why scientists try to learn when and where a natural disaster will take place. Sometimes these scientists get so close to one, they put themselves in danger.

Jeffrey Masters flies planes into **hurricanes**. Herb Stein chases **tornadoes** (tor-NAY-doze) in his special truck. Mike McPhaden watches the ocean for signs that might mean changes in the world's weather.

Scientists helped the people on one island prepare for a disaster. When a **volcano erupted**, the people were ready. The scientists had saved many lives.

Learn more about natural disasters and the important work that scientists do.

CHAPTER ONE

HUNTING HURRICANES

On September 17, 1989, a hurricane was forming over the Atlantic Ocean. A hurricane is a big storm that starts over the sea. Hurricanes have strong winds that spread out over many miles. They spin around in a huge circle. They also have lightning and rain.

This hurricane was called Hurricane Hugo.

Jeffrey Masters

Jeffrey Masters, a weather scientist, wanted to learn more about it. He and some other scientists planned to fly into the most dangerous part of the storm. The scientists call themselves hurricane hunters. They were going to fly in a special plane made to fly in rough weather.

Hurricanes have very strong winds.

The plane took off and climbed to 10,000 feet (3,048 meters). Jeffrey checked the plane's **radar** (RAY-dar) screen and saw the huge storm. It was about 300 miles (482.8 kilometers) wide. While the scientists were looking at the storm, the screen went blank.

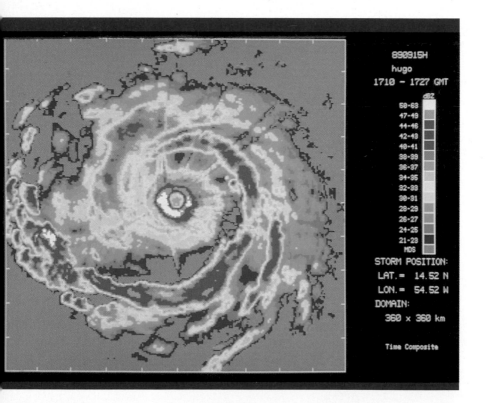

A radar map showing Hurricane Hugo's position

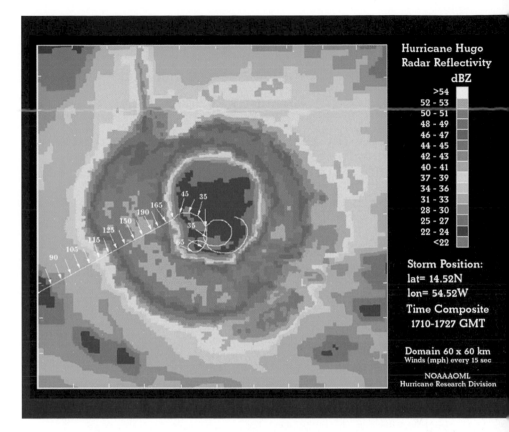

The flight path of the plane as it flew into the storm

The hurricane hunters were flying toward the storm, but they couldn't tell where they were going. Soon the plane would have to enter Hurricane Hugo. Just at that moment, the radar lit up again.

The plane flew closer to the center of the hurricane. Winds hit the plane. Heavy rains lashed at its sides. It took two pilots to control the plane. One pilot had flown into dozens of other hurricanes. This one was the worst he had ever seen.

Inside the cabin of the plane after it was hit by heavy winds

This photo shows one of the plane's engines after it has burst into flames and stopped working.

Inside the plane, the scientists measured the size of the clouds. They used radios to send these facts to the **National Hurricane Center** in Miami, Florida. At the center, other scientists used the facts that had been sent to find out which way the storm was moving. Then, they would warn people who were in the way of the storm.

As the plane was about to reach the storm's center, a strong wind hit the plane. An engine burst into flames. Would the plane make it through the storm?

Hurricane hunter airplanes are made to fly in rough weather.

A voice came over the radio. It was from an **Air Force** plane. The Air Force pilot helped Jeffrey and his team get through the storm safely.

The plane landed on the ground. The hurricane hunters had made it through the danger. They would never forget the day they flew into the powerful winds of Hurricane Hugo.

This photo was taken inside the eye of Hurricane Hugo.

The sun was shining brightly as they flew out of the storm.

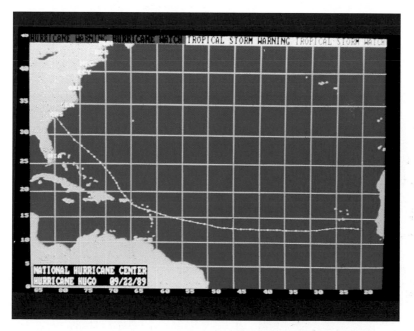

Hurricane Hugo's path

CHAPTER TWO

CHASING TORNADOES

In Oklahoma, powerful winds were tearing leaves and small branches from the trees. Herb Stein sat inside his truck. The truck weighed 13 tons. The wind was so strong, it rocked the truck back and forth. Rain poured down the windshield, making it hard to see the storm. Suddenly, there was a loud bang. Something had crashed against the side of the truck.

Herb Stein

Herb is a scientist who follows storms called tornadoes. Tornadoes have powerful spinning winds. The winds can blow up to 300 miles (483 kilometers) per hour. The storm Herb was trapped in did not turn into a tornado.

Tornadoes often form funnel-shaped clouds.

Herb travels in a special truck that has radar on it.

Still, the storm was a strong one. When the winds died down, Herb looked out the window. A telephone pole next to the truck had been bent in half.

In the United States, most tornadoes occur from April to June. During these months, Herb chases tornadoes. He wants to learn more about them. Tornadoes can cause a lot of damage. It is important to warn people when a tornado is on the way. If people are warned, they can try to protect themselves and their homes before a tornado strikes their town.

Tornadoes cause a lot of damage.

The radar takes pictures of storms.

Herb's work takes him on trips through the **Great Plains**. He travels on a special truck. The truck has radar on it. The radar takes pictures of storms before they become tornadoes. Many of these trucks are needed to find a tornado. Each truck takes pictures of a tornado from a different side. When all the views are put together, they make a complete picture.

Before Herb can chase a tornado, he has to know where to look for one. Tornadoes start in huge thunderstorms. Some large thunderstorms are called **supercells**. If a tornado starts inside one of these storms, it can be very strong.

Tornadoes are born in huge thunderstorms.

Tornadoes don't happen very often. Storm chasers might make ten trips and get to see only one tornado. They need luck, as well as skill, to see a tornado. Herb checks the weather maps. He looks for storm fronts. These are the places where tornadoes are most likely to form.

Sometimes Herb has to drive across many states to get to a storm front. One time, though, he did not. In 1999, a storm happened very close to his home. Herb found a storm and followed it toward his home in Oklahoma City. The storm formed many tornadoes. Each tornado was bigger than the last one.

The storm got close to Oklahoma City. It made a very big tornado. The tornado was 1 mile (1.6 kilometers) wide. The radar truck measured the winds in the tornado at 318 miles (483 kilometers) per hour. This set a world record! The truck was very close to the tornado. Herb stopped the truck. He got out to take a picture of the tornado. The tornado was gray and made a rumbling sound. It was raining and very windy. A large tree was picked up by the tornado. It went flying through the air.

The storm in Oklahoma City had world record-breaking winds.

The tornado destroyed thousands of homes.

The tornado continued on its way. Herb drove down the highway to catch up to it. The road was covered with small pieces of people's homes. When Herb got to Oklahoma City, the tornado was just passing through. It destroyed thousands of homes.

Herb was sad when he saw all the damage left behind. He hopes that learning more about tornadoes will help people be better protected.

CHAPTER THREE

WATCHING EL NIÑO

Mike McPhaden has a big, naughty child to watch. His child is called **El Niño** (el NEEN-yoh), which means "the boy" in Spanish. What is El Niño? It is a warming of the Pacific Ocean. El Niño affects much of the world's weather, especially when it is strong. It also affects the food supply for fish, marine animals, and sea birds of the Pacific Ocean.

Mike McPhaden

El Niño starts when the Pacific Ocean gets warmer than usual. Hot, moist air rises from the ocean, bringing powerful winds and rains. These winds change the usual weather patterns. As the warmer waters spread to the east, the weather patterns change, too.

Watching El Niño surf in California

A flooded highway in California

The warming of the ocean leads to many changes. In 1997 and 1998, there was a very powerful El Niño, the biggest of the twentieth century. The warm ocean and changing winds affected the weather all over the world. **Indonesia** (in-duh-NEE-zhuh) had huge wildfires. Floods covered many parts of South America. Parts of the United States had terrible rains. California had so much rain that some land slid into the ocean. This El Niño also caused many fish, sea birds, and marine mammals to die because there wasn't much food.

Argentina

Floods covered many parts of South America.

Ecuador

Peru

Paraguay

El Niño affected the weather all over the world.

A wildfire in Mexico

A blizzard in Peru

A drought in Indonesia

A mudslide in Ecuador

El Niño is not all bad, though. It often makes winters warmer in the Northwest and Midwest of the United States. It also reduces the number and strength of hurricanes.

El Niño takes place every two to seven years. The 1982 El Niño was a serious one. Scientists did not know it was on the way. The ocean and weather changes took them by surprise. Mike McPhaden and other scientists wanted to be ready the next time El Niño came.

They divided the Pacific Ocean into a **grid**. The grid stretched from South America to Australia. Seventy **buoys** (BOO-ees) float at points along the grid. The buoys take the temperature of the ocean. They also measure air temperature, the amount of moisture in the air, and the speed and direction of wind. Each buoy is like a floating weather station.

The facts from each buoy are sent to **satellites** in the sky. Then the satellites beam the facts to special computers on Earth.

A scientist checks for facts gathered by a buoy.

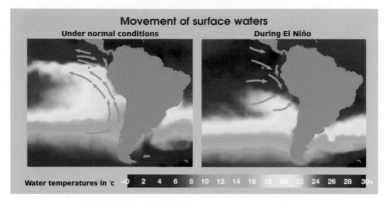

A map showing El Niño

Mike's team of scientists studies the facts. They look for changes in weather patterns. These changes might mean El Niño is coming back.

This whole **system** (SISS-tuhm) covers thousands of miles of ocean. It took Mike's team ten years to build the system. Scientists in the United States and other countries helped. The governments of the other countries help to pay for it, and it works very well. In fact, this system was used to **predict** the El Niño of 1997 and 1998.

The facts from each buoy are sent to satellites in the sky.

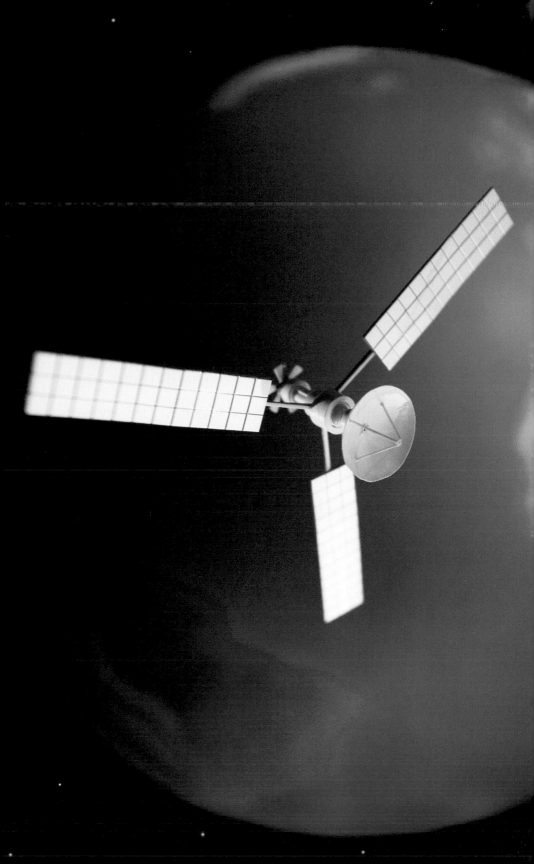

CHAPTER FOUR

STOPPING A DISASTER

Strange things were happening in the town of Rabaul in **Papua New Guinea** (PA-pyu-wuh noo GIN-ee). All during September 1994, townspeople noticed animals acting in unusual ways. Birds left their nests. Dogs barked and barked. They scratched and sniffed at the earth. Sea snakes swam to shore.

Older people in the city remembered these signs. Some of these very same things had happened nearly sixty years before. The city of Rabaul is built on a volcano. In 1937, the volcano erupted and hot **lava** (LAH-vuh) covered the land. Five hundred people died. After that, the volcano was quiet for more than forty-five years.

Rabaul, Papua New Guinea

Lava from an erupting volcano in Hawaii

Then **earthquakes** (URTH-kwayks) began to take place. Starting in 1983, thousands of earthquakes shook Rabaul. Other changes were happening, too. Hot melted rock, called **magma** (MAG-muh), was moving below Earth's surface. As the earth moved, some parts of the harbor were pushed up more than 3 feet (0.9 meters).

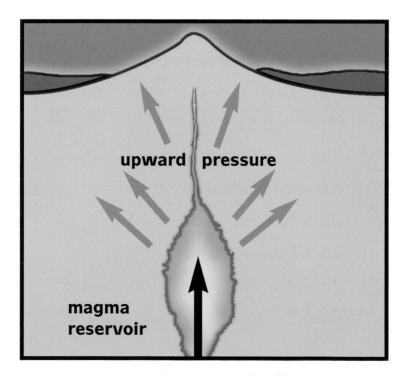

upward pressure

magma reservoir

Magma pushes up from below Earth's surface.

The town leaders knew that the volcano might erupt again. The people of Rabaul had to be ready in case it did. So leaders and scientists met with the people.

The leaders explained how the people would be warned if it seemed like the volcano would erupt. Together, they studied maps. The maps showed people how to get away safely. Finally, everyone in the town practiced an **evacuation** (i-VAK-yoo-ay-shun). The leaders made sure everyone knew where to go and what to bring with them if they had to escape.

On Sunday morning, September 18, 1994, two earthquakes were felt in the area around Rabaul. There were more earthquakes later in the day. By that night, the ocean waves were rising higher and higher.

The volcano erupting in Rabaul

The people of Rabaul began to move to safe areas. Right after the last people had escaped, the volcano erupted at the harbor. The town was badly damaged. Many homes were destroyed.

A mixture of gas and ash shoots out of the volcano.

Many people's belongings were destroyed.

Ash from the volcano covered the town like snow.

However, the plan had worked. Nearly everyone was able to get to safety. The people of Rabaul had known what to do, and they had practiced doing it. Those steps saved thousands of lives.

GLOSSARY

Air Force the part of the United States armed forces that uses planes

buoy (BOO-ee) a marker that floats in water

disaster something that causes a lot of damage

earthquake (URTH-kwayk) a movement inside Earth that causes the ground to shake

El Niño (el NEEN-yoh) the warming of the Pacific Ocean

erupt what a volcano does when it throws out lava, ash, and gas

evacuation (i-VAK-yoo-ay-shun) moving people out of danger

Great Plains an area of the west central United States and Canada

grid lines that form squares

hurricane a storm that develops over warm oceans and has powerful winds

Indonesia (in-duh-NEE-zhuh) a country in Southeast Asia

lava (LAH-vuh) hot, melted rock that flows out of volcanoes

magma (MAG-muh) hot, melted rock beneath Earth's surface

National Hurricane Center a place in Miami, Florida, where scientists study hurricanes

Papua New Guinea (PA-pyu-wuh noo GIN-ee) a country in Southeast Asia

predict to tell what will happen ahead of time

radar (RAY-dar) a machine that finds objects by using radio waves

satellite a spacecraft that circles Earth

supercell a very large thunderstorm

system (SISS-tuhm) a group of things that work together

tornado (tor-NAY-doh) a spinning column of air that comes in contact with the ground

volcano a mountain with a tube in the center through which lava, ash, and gas erupt

FIND OUT MORE

Hunting Hurricanes
www.hurricanehunters.com
Do you have a question about hurricanes? Hurricane hunters will answer them. You can read answers to other people's questions, too.

Chasing Tornadoes
www.weatherwise.org
Did you know that a tornado once lifted a train off the tracks? Read other interesting facts about tornadoes at this website.

Watching El Niño
www.nationalgeographic.com/elnino
How did El Niño get its name? Find the answer at this website.

Stopping a Disaster
www.pbs.org/wgbh/nova/vesuvius
Learn more about the Rabaul volcano and other dangerous volcanoes around the world.

INDEX

PHOTO CREDITS

MEET THE AUTHOR

 Madeline Boskey enjoys reading and writing about extreme weather, but has yet to fly into the eye of a hurricane. Boskey, a psychologist who is interested in how children learn, writes for children, parents, and teachers. She writes articles for magazines, newspapers, and websites, as well as books. The topics she has written about cover a broad range—from magic to Roman architecture to the life of Eleanor Roosevelt to the Ohio State Fair. In fact, one of the things she likes best about writing is the opportunity to learn all about a new topic. She lives with her husband and children in Summit, New Jersey.